COUNTRIES

India

Ruth Thomson

PowerKiDS press.
New York

Published in 2011 by The Rosen Publishing Group Inc.
29 East 21st Street, New York, NY 10010

First Edition

Editor: Steve White-Thomson
Designer: Amy Sparks
Picture Researchers: Ruth Thomson/
    Steve White-Thomson
Series Consultant: Kate Ruttle
Design Concept: Paul Cherrill

Library of Congress Cataloging-in-Publication Data

Thomson, Ruth, 1949-
India / by Ruth Thomson. -- 1st ed.
     p. cm. -- (Countries)
Includes index.
ISBN 978-1-4488-3276-7 (library binding)
1. India--Juvenile literature. I. Title.
DS407.T53 2011
954--dc22

                         2010023713

Photographs:
Corbis: Richard Powers front cover, Jon Hicks 5; Steve
Raymer/National Geographic Society 14; Photolibrary:
Amit Somvanshi 17, John Henry Claude Wilson 19; Neil
Thomson 23b; Shutterstock: Vishal Shah 1/9, oksana perkins
2/6r, 13, Sam DCruz 6l, 18, Igor Plotnikov 7, Luciano Mortula
8, Socrates 10, 15, Dana Ward 11, Jeremy Richards 16, 20,
Ghaint 21, Darrenp 23t, Emjay Smith 23m.

Manufactured in China
CPSIA Compliance Information: Batch #WAW1102PK: For Further Information
contact Rosen Publishing, New York, New York at 1-800-237-9932

Web Sites

Due to the changing nature of Internet
links, PowerKids Press has developed
an online list of Web sites related to
the subject of this book. This site is
updated regularly. Please use this link
to access this list:
http://www.powerkidslinks.com/cou/india

Contents

Where Is India?

Here is a map of India.

India is a huge country in Asia.

New Delhi is the capital city.

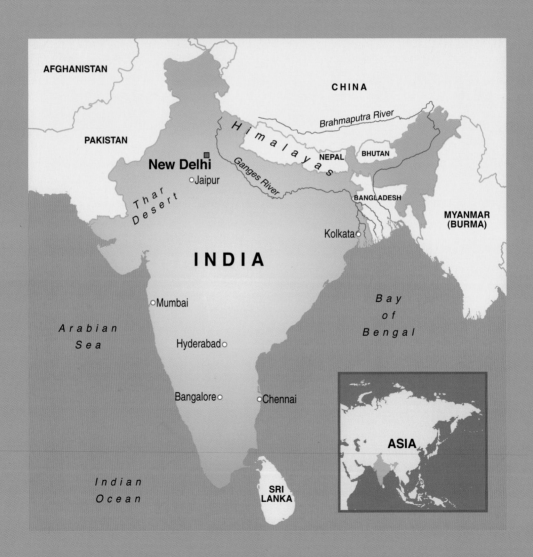

There are enormous cities in India.
These were built hundreds of years ago.
Some still have old forts and palaces.

Bangalore has many modern buildings.
Factories here make computers and aircraft parts.

Land and Sea

India has high mountains, called the Himalayas, in the north. Farther south, there are fertile plains, long rivers, and cool hills. There is a desert in the west.

The Himalayas are the highest mountains in the world.

The desert is hot and dry. It hardly ever rains there.

India has thousands of miles of coastline. The beaches are mainly sandy. In the south, palm trees grow near the shore.

Some fishermen live in villages on the beach. They build their own houses.

The Weather

India has three seasons.

Summers are hot and dry.

It is coolest in the hills.

The air is very dusty in the summer months.

After the summer, monsoon winds bring heavy rain for months. Winters are cool. It snows in the mountains.

Farmers plant rice by hand after the monsoon rains have softened the earth.

During the monsoon season, it rains every day.

Town and Country

Indian cities are very busy. The streets are full of motorcycles, autorickshaws, and buses, as well as shoppers and street traders. Cows often wander the streets, too.

Cows are seen as holy animals. No one is allowed to harm them.

autorickshaw

Many Indians live in villages.
They grow food crops. Farmers
on the plains grow wheat and rice.
Farmers in the hills grow coffee or tea.

Tea pickers pluck only the tips of tea bushes.

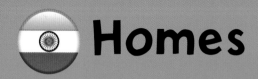

Homes

More and more Indians want to live in towns and cities. They hope for a better life there. Some Indians live in stylish houses. But the poorest people live in homemade shacks.

The city of Mumbai is home to 14 million people.

Many village houses do not have running water or electricity. Women collect water from a well and wash clothes in rivers. They cook on stoves outside.

People use wood or cow dung as fuel for cooking.

Shopping

Indians shop for fruit and vegetables in open-air markets. There are new shopping malls in big cities.

Young people enjoy shopping for clothes in malls.

Most shops are small. They do
not have shop windows. Roadside
stalls sell cheap goods or offer
services, such as watch repairs.

Indian money
is rupees.

The shopkeepers open and close
their shops when they want.

In towns, people can buy all kinds of cheap, cooked snacks from street sellers.

You can buy roti bread with spicy vegetables from this street seller.

Most Indian meals include several dishes of spicy vegetables and sauces. These are served with bread or rice.

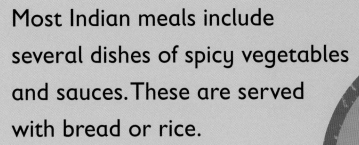

Indians make sweets from milk, flavored with chocolate, coconut, or nuts.

Some Indians eat at a table and use silverware. Many eat sitting on the floor and scoop up food with their right hand.

17

Sports and Leisure

Cricket is the most popular
sport in India. Boys play it on
any open space they can find.

Cricket is a game that is a little like baseball.
These boys play cricket on a crowded beach.

Indians enjoy watching movies. Hundreds of movies are made each year in Mumbai. The most popular movies are musicals. They have lots of songs and dances.

There is always a wide choice of movies to see at the theater.

Festivals

There are many different religions in India. Most people are Hindus, but there are also Sikhs, Muslims, Buddhists, and Christians.

Hindus pray in buildings called temples.

There are festivals throughout the year in India. Holi is a festival that celebrates the coming of spring. Diwali celebrates the Hindu New Year.

At Diwali, people light their homes with oil lamps and candles.

Speak Hindi!

Hindi is one of India's many languages. People use different Hindi words and speak with different accents depending on where they live in India.

Namaste (*Nah-mah-stay*)   Hello/ Goodbye

Kripya (*Krup-ya*)   Please

Shukriya (*Shook-ree-yah*)   Thank you

Haan (*Ha*)   Yes

Nahin (*N-he*)   No

Mera naam…hai (*Meh-ra nahm…hi*)   My name is…

The Indian flag is always made from hand-spun cotton, silk, or wool.

Indian Wildlife

India has several wildlife parks.
Big animals, such as tigers, elephants,
and rhinoceroses, live there.

The tiger lives in dense forests
and grasslands. It eats other
animals, such as deer, goats,
and boar.

The Asian elephant wanders through
forests. It eats grass, bark, and leaves.

Make a collage of
one of these animals.

Glossary and Further Information

capital the city in a country where the government is

desert a place where it scarcely rains, so the earth is very dry and few plants can grow

fertile fertile land is good for growing food crops

festival a holiday when people celebrate something special

market a place with stalls where people buy and sell things

monsoon a time when heavy rain falls

plains a large, flat area of land with few trees

season a particular time of the year

spice a plant that adds flavor to food

well a deep hole in the ground where people can get water

Books

A Visit to India
by Peter Roop
(Heinemann Library, 2008)

Facts About Countries: India
by Lizanne Flatt
(Sea to Sea Publications, 2009)

Spotlight on India
by Robin Johnson
(Crabtree Publishing Company, 2008)

Index